# Me Before You

## Jojo Moyes

### A Summary, Analysis & Review

## Note:

We encourage you to purchase the full version as this is a Summary & Analysis of Me Before You by Jojo Moyes.

The trademarks that are used are without any consent, and the publication of the trademark is without permission or backing by the trademark owner. All trademarks and brands within this book are for clarifying purposes only and are owned by the owners themselves, not affiliated with this document.

**The author or publisher are not liable for any damages whatsoever. The fact that an individual or organization is referred to in this document as a citation or source of information does not imply that the author or publisher endorses the information that the individual or organization provided.**

# TABLE OF CONTENTS

- **Introduction**
- **Book Review**
- **Character List**
- **Summary of the Chapters**
- **Discussion Questions**
- **Analysis of Themes & Symbols**
- **Analysis of Story Setting**

## -Introduction

Will Traynor had the ideal life. He was living how he wanted and loving it. Until the accident.

Louisa Clark enjoys her simple life. Then, suddenly, the café she works in closes and she finds herself without a job. Her family is struggling and really needs the income. Through the help of the Job Center, Louisa gets an interview to be a care taker. Not her ideal job, but it pays well.

Will and Louisa despise one another at first. However, as time goes on, Will becomes determined to make Louisa see the potential she is shutting away by not getting out there.

One day, Louisa finds out the terrible reason why she is there. Can she go on with the charade? Can she watch someone who she has learned to care about do this to himself?

*Me Before You* is a compelling novel about how a life can suddenly be changed in an instant. The trials and heartbreaks show Louisa that she really is meant for more...

**-Book Overview**

After Will's accident, he is paralyzed from the neck down. He is forced to move in with his parents. One day, he knows that this wasn't the life that he was meant to live and tries to take his life. In a hope that Will can be enticed to change his mind, Camilla Traynor, his mother, hires someone who is meant to cheer him up. She has six months to change his mind.

As time goes on, Will and Louisa become close friends. Louisa even finds that she is falling for him. However, her heart is broken when nothing she could do will change his mind to go through the plan that will end his life.

**-Main and Secondary List of Characters**

## Main Characters

Louisa Clark

William Traynor

Katrina Clark

Camilla Traynor

Steven Traynor

Nathan

## Secondary Characters

Josie Clark

Patrick

Thomas Clark

Alicia Witte

Bernard Clark

**-Summary of the Chapters (With Some Analytical Comments Interspersed)**

Prologue

We get a brief insight into the life that Will Traynor lived before his accident. He has a lovely woman he adored and a job that he was in total control in. Then the motorbike came around the corner and there was no way to avoid being hit...

1-2

Louisa knows every detail of her life and likes it just the way it is. However, her life is changing today. She was told that her boss was shutting down the café that she had worked in for the past six years. With her income being depended upon, she has no idea where the future is going.

She enrolls in the Career Center and ends up with a few jobs, but none of them suit her at all. Her advisor is about to give up hope when a new position pops up. A caregiver. Louisa is adamant that she will not clean old people's bottoms. However, it's her last resort, the money is good, and she really needs to come through for the family.

Josie lends her a suit for the interview with Camilla Traynor. From the beginning, Louisa is uneasy and sure that she is not qualified for the job that she is interviewing for. Granta House, the home of the Traynors, is intimidating. She finds that the interview is tense, but she is surprised when she is offered the job. Of course she will take it!

3-4

Louisa starts her job the next morning. Will lives in the annex of the house, which was converted into a comfortable living space for his wheelchair. Camilla shows her around and leaves Nathan to tell her about the procedures and the medications that she is expected to give Will.

Will is less than cooperative from the beginning. He starts out by trying to scare Louisa away. Everything he does makes Louisa feel inadequate. She really hates that job and wishes that the six month contract would end. In an effort to feel needed, she cleans the annex over and over again. That is when she gets a glimpse of Will's former life. The skiing, the mountain climbing. She begins to understand why Will is mean and bitter.

After the first day, Treena (Katrina) tells her that she wishes to go back to school. She and her son, Thomas, will start in a few weeks.

Alicia, Will's ex-girlfriend, and Rupert, his old colleague, show up at the annex to announce that they are going to get married. Will seems to take this in stride, but Alicia was his love and the thought of her marrying another man devastated him.

5-6

Louisa is unsettled by the demeanor of Camilla Traynor. Nothing she does seems to be right in her employer's eyes. She continues on, but she feels like she is being scrutinized at every turn.

Nathan, Will's nurse, is the first to notice a change in Will's mood. He tells Louisa that he seems happier and talks more since she has been around. She finds that she is spending more and more time with Will and actually enjoying it. She starts to watch films with him and begins to read books in his collection.

Will attempts to get to know her better. By asking her questions, he determines that she leads a limited life and her only entertainment is a boyfriend who does nothing but run. He just cannot fathom how she can live like that.

After a doctor's appointment, Louisa realizes he truth about Will's condition. He will never get better, no matter what. She realizes what Will has known for some time.

A few days later, Louisa finds herself stuck with Will during a blizzard. And Will is very ill. She does what she can to make him comfortable, but he just seems to be getting worse. When Nathan arrives, he is upset to know that Will has been in that condition for hours. He gives him medication to help him regulate his body temperature.

Louisa is all but stranded at Granta House. She is concerned and upset about what had happened to Will that morning. She tells her mother that she will stay the night. Louisa never leaves his side the entire night. After Will begins to feel better, they discuss more about one another, such as Louisa's odd taste in clothing.

7-8

Will continues to question Louisa's simple life. He cannot understand how she can be content in a simple world. After a tirade about how she made the tea too strong, Will asks her to express her opinions. And she does. She tells him that he looks homeless with the unkempt hair and facial hair. Laughing, he agrees to let her shave him and cut his unruly hair.

As she is finishing, Georgina, Will's sister comes into the room and lets loose on how selfish he is. A while later, Louisa hears a private conversation between Camilla and Georgina and finds out that Will had tried to commit suicide and had asked for their blessings in an assisted suicide. That is why Louisa had been hired. To keep an eye on him and change his mind.

When they had found Will after his first attempt, Camilla had been reluctant to agree to Will's request. She would not aid her son to his death. She asked him to give it six months before he tried anything else. He gave her his word. Her next thought was was how she could change his mind.

9-11

Louisa doesn't know if she can be a pawn in the plan. She feels like she has been lied to. The next day, she is prepared to hand in her resignation. Camilla is shocked and begs her to stay. She follows Louisa home to discuss the situation. She will double the salary. Louisa has been good for Will and she cannot let that go.

Treena talks Louisa into returning to the job. She says that it is a challenge and that she should do whatever she can to make Will change his mind. After drinking a bottle of wine, the girls decide to find activities that will show Will that there is still life in a wheelchair. The next morning, Louisa spells out her plans for the Traynors. They are desperate to try anything and agree.

Katrina prepares to leave for school the next week. Their mother misses her greatly and things are just not the same without her and Thomas. Louisa begins going to the library to research activities that Will can do.

The first outing is a horse race. This turns into a disaster as Will's chair gets stuck in mud, they are unable to eat at the restaurant, and a bunch of drunk men help him back to the car. It is once they return home that Will tells her that he hates horses and always has.

12

Louisa flashes back to a time where she was just like the rest of the girls. She took a job at the car park near the town's castle and ended up in the company of some men who were less than honest. She got drunk and high that night and does not remember what had happened in the maze. All she knows is that she doesn't want to go back to that maze ever again.

Will tells her that his plays violin in an orchestra and has given him tickets to a performance. He invites Louisa to go with him. She is reluctant, as she has never listened to classical music. However, for Will, she agrees to get dressed up and go with him. She agrees to do the bedtime routine for him and everything. If this is something Will will enjoy, she is going to do it.

She finds that the evening goes really well. She enjoys the performance and Will does as well.

13-15

Louisa finds ways in which Will can use a computer. Camilla is more than willing to let her install it on Will's computer, and Will actually begins using it. He writes letters and reads the news without assistance.

Louisa lets her mother cook dinner for her birthday. She invites Will over, along with Patrick. She is afraid that Will will turn down the invitation, but to her astonishment, he agrees to come to her birthday party.

Will is very endearing to Louisa's family. She can also see that Patrick is becoming jealous of her friendship with Will. She loves his gift more than the one Patrick gave her, and that makes him angry.

The next month, assisted suicide became a huge news topic. Watching it made her feel even more desperate to save Will. Then her father lost his job. Now, the family was totally dependent on Louisa's wages.

Louisa tries as discreetly as she can to think up ideas for taking Will out of the house. She asks him about his adventures. Since Will seems more concerned in furthering her life, she makes him tell her that she has to see herself doing these things. He finally mentions a café in Paris. Delighted, Louisa tells him they could go. However, he shuts down the idea immediately. That was a place from his past life and he didn't want to go back to it in a wheelchair.

Mrs. Traynor is pushing for Louisa to take William abroad. She says she will pay for everything. Even though she hates to admit it, all of Will's improvements are because of Louisa. She wants Louisa to continue what she's doing in order to achieve changes.

Louisa is upset that Will thinks that she has a boring life and never does anything fun. A bet between him and Nathan proves that. He had lived a big life and didn't regret it. He just wants Louisa to experience life outside of that small town.

When Will ends up in the hospital, Louisa takes to the library to find chatrooms that will help her with her plight. She is pleased to discover that there are many people out there in Will's condition and still enjoying life. She holds onto that and asks them advice as to how she can change his mind about what he wants to do to himself.

Once out, Louisa tries to get him to try more activities. After a wine tasting that he had enjoyed and she hadn't, Will convinces her to get a tattoo as they drive home. She knows her family will hate it, but she takes the chance. And loves it.

16-17

In a discussion with Will, Louisa reveals her home problems, mainly that her father has lost his job. A few days later, she finds that Will's father has hired him for maintenance around the castle. The family is no longer the only wage earner. She is happy for her dad, but upset that Will would pull strings for her. She wasn't' asking for favors.

With the sleeping arrangements at home being difficult to cope with, Patrick invites Louisa to move in with him. Will had also offered a place for the weekends. However, Louisa had been with Patrick for six years and figures that this is the next step in their relationship. Will is upset by the turn of events, even though he will not admit it.

A lawyer shows up at the annex one day and he and Will have a long talk. After she gets off, Louisa goes to the library and finds out that this lawyer specializes in wills. Nothing she has done yet has changed his mind.

Mrs. Traynor and Louisa have a conversation about the developments in the plan at a café near the castle. When Louisa reveals that she has moved in with her boyfriend, Mrs. Traynor is livid. She knows that Will likes Louisa and fears that this turn of events will be a setback. Louisa is also upset that Mrs. Traynor is trying to control her life.

Louisa feels herself drifting away from Will. She takes the cleaning more seriously than before and she avoids him. One night, he tells her that his father has given him the keys to the castle and that they can roam it without the tourists. Will wants to go into the maze, as it had been an obstacle for him as a child. Louisa balks, but she doesn't want to disappoint Will with the reason why she hates the maze. After getting lost in there, flashbacks haunt her about the night she had lost her fearlessness in there. When Will finds her, she tells him the story of what happened. Now he understands what keeps her from branching out. She's afraid.

18-21

Will decides to go to Alicia's wedding with Louisa as his guest. As they "dance," Louisa gets will to agree to go away with her. She has met a friend of his who is willing to help her get into a retraining program, which interests her greatly. They have a marvelous time, except Louisa gets drunk and is unable to care for his needs, making him ill. Will warns Nathan not to say anything to her because she had the time of her life.

Louisa plans an amazing trip for Will where he can do some of the adventurous things he was used to in his past life. The quads online had helped her find the place. She carefully makes all the plans and Mrs. Traynor approves them. She then presents them to everyone, and Will agrees to go.

After Louisa tells Patrick she will not support him for a triathlon to go on this trip, they break up. It has become apparent to Patrick that she has feelings for Will. She subsequently moves into the annex.

22-24

Will gets pneumonia a week before the trip and all the plans have to be cancelled. This is depressing for Louisa, but she is still determined to get him away from home. She has been talking to a quadriplegic man on line by the name of Ritchie, who has an uncle who is a travel agent. He calls her and sets up an alternative vacation that Will is sure to enjoy.

After a twelve hour flight, they are in Mauritius, a place Will had loved to go before his accident. Louisa is enamored by the beauty of the area. While Will rests, she lays by his side and watches the ocean. He encourages her to try new things. Even after trying some water sports, she finds that she is still content to lie next to Will on the beach.

On the last day, she tries scuba diving. This is an adventure like nothing else, and it lifts her spirits. She feels wonderful that night and decides to let loose at dinner. Afterwards, she takes Will down to the beach where she tells him that they could build a life together just as he is. He then tells her that nothing will change his mind about the assisted suicide. He had made his mind up and that he hopes that she will continue to expand her life once he is gone.

Louisa is furious and refuses to speak to him all the way home. At the airport, she tells him mother of his continued plan and leaves the job.

25-27

Louisa is incredibly depressed once she returns home. After a few days, she finally tells Katrina what had happened. Then all hell breaks loose when they find out that the media had found out about Will's plans. Patrick had told them for money. While screening answering machine calls, Katrina finds one from Mrs. Traynor, begging Louisa to call her.

Will wants Louisa to be with him in Switzerland, where he plans the end of his life. Louisa agrees to go and is met by her parents as she gets ready to leave for the airport. Her mother is insistent that she should have no part in this and that if she goes, she is not welcome at home. Louisa goes anyway.

The last moments she spends with Will are heartbreaking. He tells her that he hopes that he has changed her life for the better and that she continues to expand her horizons.

Since Will had made his attentions known and had made all his final plans, there was no legal involvement in his death.

Epilogue

Will had left Louisa money. The first place he wanted her to go was the French café that he had spoken on. Opening his letter, she finds out that he has left her enough money to cover her expenses for college for the next four years.

He wants her to succeed, no matter what has happened.

**-Thought Provoking/or Discussion Questions for both Readers & Book Clubs**

Louisa lives in England. When she loses her job, she goes a different route to find a new one than you may. How would you handle her situation?

If confronted with a person such as Will, how would you react?

Upon finding out the plans, what would you say and do?

Would you support a loved one's decision to do what Will did?

**-Discussion & Analysis of Themes, Symbols ...**

Adventure seems to be the key theme I this book.  While Will had lived a lifetime of adventure before his accident, Louisa had remained safe.  As Will prepares to die, he wants to show Louisa that being adventurous is not bad. As a life ends, a new adventure begins.

**-Story Setting Analysis**

While Will's accident happens in London, the bulk of the story takes place in Tenby, England. This small town houses a historical castle that draws tourists in the summer.  This is a small, secluded area which Louisa has never really ventured from.

In Tenby, Will feels stuck.  He got away from it when he was younger, and now he is back again against his will.  He wants to see Louisa break away from its confines as well.

As the story progresses, Louisa does get to see more of the world.  She goes to Mauritius with Will and Nathan.  She also goes to Switzerland to spend the last few hours of Will's life with him.

While the story starts in the small town, it ends by setting Louisa free from the bonds that the town has had on her her entire life. She has found her wings.

# Leopard Books Author Page

Leopard Books, is your perfect quick read companion.

We analyze every chapter and hunt down the key points for your convenience.

With in-depth summary and analysis, leap through books quickly and with ease.

CPSIA information can be obtained at www.ICGtesting.com
Printed in the USA
LVOW10s0234080416

482718LV00021B/350/P